2021 Edition

HOW TO TALK SO HE WILL LISTEN

And

LISTEN SO HE WILL TALK

12 Steps To Better Love Relationships For Women

Jacquelyn Elnor Johnson

©2016, 2021 Crimson Hill Books/Crimson Hill Products Inc.

All rights reserved. No part of this book, including words and illustrations may be copied, lent, excerpted or quoted except in very brief passages by a reviewer.

Cataloguing in Publication Data

Jacquelyn Elnor Johnson

How To Talk So He Will Listen And Listen So He Will Talk

Description: Crimson Hill Books trade paperback edition | Nova Scotia, Canada

ISBN: 978-1-989595-71-8 (Paperback - Ingram)

BISAC: FAMILY & RELATIONSHIPS/General
FAMILY & RELATIONSHIPS/Love & Romance
FAMILY & RELATIONSHIPS/Marriage & Long-Term Relationships

THEMA: Popular beliefs & controversial knowledge
Relationships and families: advice and issues
Practical advice: Life hacks / handy tips

Record available at https://www.bac-lac.gc.ca/eng/Pages/home.aspx

Book Design & Formatting: Jesse Johnson

This book was previously published as Talk So He Will Listen in 2012 and was revised in 2016. This is the third, revised edition.

Crimson Hill Books
(a division of)
Crimson Hill Products Inc.
Wolfville, Nova Scotia
Canada

Introduction to this 2021 Edition

You could call this the Talking & Listening To Men Success Guide.

Though revised, it remains a fast read on purpose, to quickly give you insights and simple techniques you can put into action immediately.

Effective communication is the key that can open so many doors in life. It can also help get you to that place of true intimacy and understanding with the one (and ones) you love.

Good conversation skills are the first step to listening, respecting and caring for others and earning their respect, caring (and possibly love) in return. These skills can help you gain success in business, in any social situation and, most importantly, in your personal life.

It's my aim in this book to help you feel much more comfortable the next time you have a conversation with any man who is important to you, whether he is your boyfriend, husband, father, brother, son, uncle, nephew, friend, boss, colleague, client, student or any other boy or man in your life.

Here's to good conversations!

Jacquelyn Elnor Johnson
Greenwich, NS, October 2020

Here's what readers have to say about this book:

Dives deep into body language, situations, timing of conversations. Also breaks down how to (and how not to) handle situations with people no matter their relationship to you. This is a very effective communication handbook.
- Joseph C., Amazon reader

I wished there was a book like this years ago :-) It would have saved me a lot of thinking about what he had meant by this or that.

The book could also help you if you are starting your career, since many of the principles apply in the corporate world when talking to your boss, regardless if male or female. And colleagues as well.
- Francesca, Amazon reader

My wife and I will be married nine years this August, and it seems communication this past year had begun breaking down between us.

She read this book and asked me to read it, too. The book is written for women, but since she asked me to read it, and it looked like a quick read, I figured what the heck.

However, for me, the book was eye-opening. Really struck a chord with me and my wife. Definitely recommended for couples who've been together for years.
- Rick, Amazon reader

Ok, well written book, I get the difference now. Honestly, this book helps me recognize we really do speak different languages.

If nothing else, it makes me open my mind, listen more and understand what's being said by my better half. As

much as I regret to admit it.... Great Job Jackie. I get it now lol.
— The Gull Lake Guy, Amazon Reader

This is one of those books that I wish I had read a long time ago, when I was starting out trying to communicate with men. I thought I knew how to do that but after reading this book, I realize that what I knew about was communicating with women.

I've always expected men to respond to conversations the way my girlfriends do. From ex's to bosses to lovers, this book breaks down men's needs in conversations. Very valuable.
— Helen C. Page, Amazon reader

This book is valuable for not only people in a love relationship but for anyone who feels like they aren't being heard by the people in their lives. I actually feel like I now have a secret advantage over others for knowing how to be effectively heard and for making all of my relationships work!
— Raphael G., Amazon reader

A quick read with tips that make sense. Maybe they're tips I could've figured out for myself, but I haven't yet so I guess it just helps to have them listed and probed a little. I could relate to the author's assessments and observations and appreciated the strategies--some of which are familiar, but all of which bear being reminded about.
— Carol Zakula, Amazon reader

Reviews are taken from Amazon.com for the first and second editions of this book and have been edited for length.

Contents

Introduction to This 2021 Edition 3
Chapter 1 – We Have to Talk About Talking and Listening 9
Chapter 2 - How to Talk and Know He's Listening to You 15
Chapter 3 - What Is Good Talk? 31
Chapter 4 - Recognize The Conversation Killers . . . 55
Chapter 5 - Who HE Is Matters 91
Chapter 6 - Don't Make These Common Listening Mistakes! 97
Chapter 7 - Reading His Signals 107
Chapter 8 - Where's This Going? 115
Chapter 9 - You Had Me At "Hello" 123
Chapter 10 - Keep The Conversation Rolling Along . 129
Chapter 11 - Happy Endings 141
Chapter 12 - Exit Smiling. 144
Chapter 13 - Advanced Skillset 1 – Dealing With Difficult Topics. 147
Chapter 14 - Advanced Skillset 2 – Dealing With Difficult Men 151
Chapter 15 - Wishing You Many Happy Conversations... 155

How To Talk So He Will Listen

Chapter One

We Have To Talk About Talking And Listening

How often have you found yourself trying to talk to the man who matters most in your life, but he doesn't seem to be listening?

Instead, his eyes keep drifting to the TV screen. Or his phone. Or he's looking everywhere except at you.

I bet he hasn't heard a word I'm saying, you think to yourself.

So why not?

Doesn't he care about you and what you have to say?

Doesn't he want to understand you and what you want and need?

And just why is he so distracted?

Is he just stressed? Tired? Bored?

Or could it be he's thinking of something else...or someone else?

How can you get him to listen when you talk...and reveal what he's really thinking when he talks to you?

This book is written for any woman who wants a deeper, richer, closer and more loving relationship with the significant man in her life, or the man she wants to attract into her life soon.

If you are this woman, you really want to talk to your man, listen to him and communicate with him, on a deep and meaningful level.

You want to understand him.

You need to trust him.

And you want him to want and need to both listen and talk to you.

Really talk.

Really listen.

You want the quality communication that starts – or continues – to build a warm and satisfying loving relationship with your man; a relationship of trust and devotion that can last a lifetime.

This book provides insights, tips and tools that can be used to improve any relationship, but the focus is on using communication skills to create a better, more loving relationship between a man and a woman.

You may say that talking to your lover and listening to him just comes naturally if you truly love each other.

Or that two people who are attracted to each other will just naturally know what to say. If he truly is Mr. Right, (not just Mr. Right Now or even Mr. Good Enough), everything will be easy and right between you from the first moment you meet. He'll just automatically be the best talker, the best listener, the best kisser you've ever known. And, of course, the sex will be sensational; the best you've ever known.

Or maybe you believe that anyone can talk and listen because good communication skills are just good old common sense.

Or that we're all pretty good communicators. After all, we've been talking and listening just about all our lives.

But anyone who has reached adulthood has already learned that common sense truly isn't all that common.

People aren't born with these skills in living and loving. They must be learned.

For many reasons, good communication skills don't come easily to most of us.

This also has to be learned.

If you were not one of those few lucky people who had the advantage of growing up in a happy, loving and supportive home, raised by people who knew how to love each other and show it in all the ways they communicated, what you will have learned are the lessons of needs not met and of dysfunction. This includes having learned some poor communicating habits and poor ways of relating to people, including those you love or are supposed to love. Or want to love.

You may have some un-learning to do

When you grow up in a non-loving or non-communicating family or without family (as, sadly, too many people do), or are the ongoing target of bullying or discrimination, you have a harder time learning anything positive. Not only is your social learning slowed down or stunted, but recent research is also showing that enduring the extremes of non-loving, that is abuse, neglect or violence, can actually make changes to your brain.

At the same time, when this happens in childhood, you are not learning those critical lessons about getting along in life including how to trust, how to love and how to communicate in positive ways.

The good news is just about everyone can improve in both social skills and loving skills, regardless of what happened in the past.

We have the ability to replace poor habits with better ones, or bad information with what's true and good.

Loving well is a skill, like any other.

We can all be better talkers, better listeners and better lovers to the ones we choose to love.

If this is what you want – a happier, richer, more fulfilling relationship with the man you love, or the man you want to attract into your life, grab a coffee (or a glass of wine), get comfortable and let's *really* talk about talking and listening to the man you love...and how to get what you want and need in your communicating life and in your love life.

It all starts with a good conversation.

This one

Chapter Two

How To Talk And Know He's Listening To You

Cast your mind back to before you knew how to talk, or even babble in baby talk, or cry for what you wanted.

Can you remember that time in your life?

For almost everyone, the answer has to be *No*.

Communicating to get what we want and need from the people closest to us is a skill studied and then practiced so early in life that we really don't remember how we learned to do it.

It just happens. Naturally, or so we believe. After all, every infant human does this.

Generally, as women, we think this Talk/Listen thing is easy and, as women, we're all good at it. In Western cultures, girls are encouraged to talk – a lot – with other girls and women. We grow up talking because girls are taught that the meaning of life is relationships. That requires talking and listening.

When women get together there is usually plenty of communicating going on. And about some things (such as the people in our lives, our current projects, our kids, our pets, our hopes and dreams and desires and worries and fears) the talk rarely stops. It flows all around us, like a great river of communication, all our lives.

Also, as women talking to other women, we rarely have difficulty working out 'what she really meant by that.'

We live in a culture that raises girls to be concerned with nurturing and relationships and talk about them to each other. Boys, we are taught, aren't at all interested in "all that girl stuff."

Even though the world-view female children are taught is that everything is about relationships. How we relate, to whom, is the entire meaning of life.

Girls talk; boys do. Boys are raised to strive. To take action. To express big ambitions. To slay dragons. Everyone knows this.

Do you recall all those scenes in *Sex And The City* and what the girlfriends were talking about? Sometimes, it was career challenges and very briefly it was about real estate (Carrie finally bought her apartment). Girl décor, that is shoes, beauty and fashion, got a lot of attention.

But most of the time, those four women were talking about the men in their lives, and what did he mean when he said …? Or did…? Or didn't …? And could he be thinking about…or planning to ask…or avoiding asking…or…?

These topics never got old with the women in this show.

Women talk in different ways, and for different reasons than men do.

Did all that talk about talking to men seem endless to you? Or did it just sound like the way women talk when we're together?

Like the countless conversations you've overheard or been a part of, involving women regarding men.

Is talking to men truly THAT fascinating? Or is it that we just keep trying to 'get it?' and 'do it right,' or at least better?

Is it that we see men and how they communicate with us as a puzzle to be solved? Or a treasure chest to be unlocked?

Are men secret-holders, mostly denying women access to their true feelings?

Or do they truly just not care but only say what they think we want to hear when it suits them?

When women and men attempt to communicate, the confusion can sometimes be profound.

Even though you are both (or all) speaking the same language, the fact is men and women DO communicate differently. Part of this is the way we're brought up, but part of it is also the ways our brains work.

If you're talking to men as if you're talking to your girlfriends, STOP right now! Men DO talk – and think – differently than we do!

Just like us, men have grown up with rules about talking – how, when, to whom, what about.

This book is about how to talk to men and how to be listened to by men in a manner that is clearer for everyone. It will give you some simple tools you can use to communicate with THE man in your life, in a way that is honest, clear and amazingly effective.

By effective, I don't mean controlling or manipulative. Effective communication is when message sent = message received.

There's no cause for misunderstanding.

I've broken it down into 12 steps in this short, practical book. Master each one, and you'll be the woman people (including men) want to talk to, and listen to.

You will be able to do this because you will finally have those insights into the ways women communicate, and the ways men communicate, and how (and why) they are different. This book isn't meant to be the final word on the subject – but it will do more than get you started and may be all you need to improve all your relationships, but particularly the one at the center of your life.

It isn't that one gender's style is better or more effective than the other, merely that they are different.

Apples or oranges. White wine or red. Coffee or tea. London or Paris.

Each wonderful and distinctively different.

Imagine for a moment what it would be like to be in a relationship where you both communicate clearly and understand each other, just about all the time.

Would that be worth a bit of effort to get?

Imagine cutting down (even eliminating most of) the misunderstandings, arguments, confusion and hurt feelings. It could make some significant changes in your life...

This is a win-win strategy to speak and be heard as well as valued and respected by the significant other in your life.

You may object that it is over-simplifying to say, "All men communicate this way…" or "All women talk and listen that way" and, of course, you are right. There are individual differences.

There are men who are skilled at saying exactly what they *feel* as well as what they *think*, though I believe they're a rare breed. Certainly, there are women who are wretchedly poor communicators. Gender doesn't provide the skills, even when they are culturally taught, encouraged and endlessly reinforced.

We all live on a communication-skill continuum, with dreadfully inept at one end and brilliant at the other. This is good news because anyone can 'move on up' to being a better communicator.

Men And Women Have More In Common Than They Have Differences

Here's what's undeniable:

- We all have different levels of skill at relating to others.

- We all have different personalities.

- We are all shaped by how and where we grew up. And when.

There are, of course, other influences.

However, there are, in general, some basic differences in the way men talk and listen, and the way women do that are universal.

Partly, this is cultural – our society and the way we are raised within that society. But it also has to do with biology, brain functioning and the fact that men and women simply are not the same (and who would want them to be?). So why would communication be precisely the same?

If you doubt this, all you need to do is listen in on an all-male conversation and observe the body language as well as what is said (or not said).

Go ahead – eavesdrop. It's for a good cause (your understanding).

Consider what they talk about. How much eye contact is there? Short sentences? Longer? What subjects do they discuss? What kinds of words do they use? How many 'thinking' words are used and how many 'feeling' words are there? Note the eye contact made and the body language.

Now, repeat this exercise, but with any group of women.

It's a basic truth that due to gender, but also due to culture and other influences, women talk differently, and for different reasons, than do men.

We also listen differently.

Not all men absolutely fit the pattern of man-talk I have portrayed and not all women fit the female version. It could be that those who don't (of both genders) have learned to modify how they communicate, depending on their audience – and this is another tip in how to communicate effectively. You do have to talk in a different way, and listen in a different way, depending on the needs of the listener, who they are and <u>who they are to you</u>.

What sometimes gets in the way of our ability to understand the man we are trying to communicate with and prevents him from understanding us is simply not recognizing these few but critical differences between the two genders.

Here is a story a friend told me:

I almost missed having the conversation that would change my life, all because I was not comfortable or skilled at talking with and to men.

Let me give you the background to this story. I spent my summers, as a kid, at a beautiful luxury resort in the Rockies. Our family wasn't wealthy, but we were happy. Both my parents worked at that resort. As Dad was the manager, we got to live in a cottage on the grounds.

I would spend my summers riding horses, helping to look after the hunting dogs my family raised and, when I was older, working in the restaurant and as a lifeguard at the pool. It was a wonderful way to grow up for me and my sisters and I have many happy memories.

A few years after graduation – by this time I'd finished college and was working in a city -- I received an invitation to attend a banquet in my Dad's honor because he was retiring. I was thrilled. I was also more than a bit nervous. I knew there would be some 'high-powered' people there (my Dad was quite well-known and respected in resort management). I was afraid I would be way out of my league.

Going to 'big' events, such as this retirement party, with some of the top brass from this resort chain and the even bigger company that owns it is the kind of event that is pretty far outside my regular life and, frankly, outside my comfort zone.

But I was determined to enjoy myself and to make my Dad proud, especially since neither of my sisters could be there. I ended up having a great time and I know my Dad did as well.

When I first arrived at the banquet, I was surprised to realize that I was one of only a few women present. I'd expected there to be more people including more women, but that wasn't the case. As it was still true then that most of the senior managers of that company are male, the room was almost all men. Talk about a fancy 'guy's night out!'

After hugging my Dad and getting a few introductions, I left to make the rounds. My first stop, of course, was my Dad's boss. He had not seen me in several years, so he was surprised, as he said, that I am now, "All grown up." He went on and on about the gawky little kid and rather shy teenager I used to be.

This was my Dad's boss and my Dad's special night, so I swallowed the desire to remind this man that I am an adult now with a responsible job and simply smiled and thanked him. As soon as it was polite, I excused myself to go and speak to others.

As I walked away, I heard several groups of men talking about things that either I know little about (the hospitality industry, tourism in that part of the country, politics) or are of zero interest to me (football, oil pipelines, hunting).

I was starting to feel isolated and awkward when I heard two men talking about their bird (hunting) dogs and the newest pup one of them had just purchased.

I smiled, took a deep breath to relax and introduced myself. I explained that I was familiar with bird dogs (it's a passion of mine and the type of dogs our family had) and I had heard good things about that puppy's breed.

I had also heard about a few problems that some people who own this breed have had, and how to deal with these problems if they should occur.

We started talking more and more about dogs and our love for them and training them correctly and I found myself relaxing even more and enjoying the conversation.

The next thing I knew, I was the center of attention in this group of men and I was answering questions and giving advice about hunting dogs, left and right.

I remember at one point, catching my Dad's eye and he smiled at me; he seemed pretty pleased that I was holding my own in a room full of some pretty high-powered men, almost all of them with more life experience than me.

One of the younger men approached me afterword and introduced himself. We'd met years earlier as teenagers one summer at the resort, but we hadn't been boyfriend and girlfriend back then, just two kids who knew each other because of our summer jobs. Now, as an adult, I honestly hadn't recognized him.

He asked me a couple of specific questions about dogs and then the conversation just naturally moved to other topics. He asked if I would like to continue the conversation at one of the little tables set up out on the patio next to the pool (it was a mild, starry evening).

Talking to him seemed so easy. Finally, and reluctantly, I said I should get back to the party, but before I went inside this pleasant and interesting man asked me out to dinner the next night (he was only in town for one more day).

And I said, "Yes."

We got married the following summer.

My point in telling you this is that, if I'd gone with my first instinct (all that self-consciousness and nervousness about what do I, a young adult, have to say to these colleagues and high-flyer businessmen?) and not gone to my Dad's retirement do, I might have missed out on an enjoyable evening, marking a special event in Dad's life and reconnecting with the wonderful man I married.

Did I find my love by talking and listening? Possibly not, but that's where it started…

What About BIG Differences? Do Opposites Attract?

Opposites do at times attract – but having *enough* in common beyond your love for each other is what leads to long-term happiness for most couples.

That isn't to say that a couple with major differences in culture, background, spiritual beliefs, health or other realities in their lives won't be able to communicate successfully, because they can. And they'll need to because a marriage of 'opposites' just takes more effort from both partners.

Karla has three university degrees and was involved in a professional career when she married Jason, a man who was a trade journeyman, with a blue-collar background.

They grew up in different social classes – for her, comfortably middle class. For him, a family that struggled at times to keep food on the table and the power turned on. She was Jewish, he was Catholic. She loved city life; he preferred small towns.

They had two completely different approaches to how to use and save money...and the 'opposites' didn't end there.

Friends and family on both sides feared this marriage couldn't possibly last, yet these two went ahead and got married, twice. Once in church, once in synagogue. Many of their friends and family members have divorced and some re-married over the three decades these two have been together. You can say they were opposites, and in many ways, they still are, but they made it work.

If you are in love with an 'opposite' man, you could, too.

Good talk, and good listening, could become one of the greatest strengths you share and one of the ways you express your love for each other.

Chapter Three
Step 1: What Is Good Talk?

How are men and women different in the ways we talk and listen?

To understand this, first let's consider the way we're brought up. Children quickly learn that:

- Boys don't cry, don't express emotions in words, don't openly show affection, and are supposed to be 'strong' all the time, and 'fearless.'

- Girls can cry, hug, kiss, laugh, talk about feelings, demonstrate affection, and aren't supposed to be 'strong.' For girls, it's OK to have fears and ask for help.

- What is expected in boys – standing up for yourself, being assertive, being competitive, being independent, striving for success – is still, by and large, discouraged in girls who are so often accused of being aggressive when they are either competitive or openly ambitious.

- Boys are usually belittled when they express emotions or prefer talking to taking action.

In spite of all the battles fought to win the vote, to win equality, to legislate 'fairness,' and in spite of all the liberal, well-meaning parents who buy dolls for their boys and water-guns for their girls … despite decades of feminism … despite all the oceans of print and billions of words online about equal pay and equal opportunity as well as equal education, the absolute bottom line is this:

- We all want to be treated well.

- We all want to be happy.

- We all deserve equal rights and opportunities, but the Real World doesn't deliver that – not yet.

- We're different, and that needs to be acknowledged and celebrated, not denied.

The roles are certainly not as rigid as they once were, but we still have certain expectations about gender norms that we pass on to our children and that our society reinforces.

It is true that these gender roles are less rigid, in some ways, than in the past, but they aren't gone and likely never will be.

Men and woman communicate differently and have different interests, only in part because these are what is 'allowed' for each gender.

Women also tend to express their emotions more freely than men because it is 'allowed,' not because we are born that way. These are socially- and culturally- encouraged gender roles.

So, what else can we say about these differences?

One major difference in the way men and women communicate is that women tend to be able to talk about most subjects equally, no matter who we are with or what gender the audience is.

Men talk very differently with other men than they do around women and particularly when alone with one woman. Men do this without thinking about it. It's just automatic to adjust to the gender of the audience for most men.

Men rarely have problems talking to other men. Few men feel confident, always, talking to women.

How Men Talk, What Women Hear

Men tend to talk to each other about their interests, just like women do. The big difference is that their interests are, in general, quite different from those of most women.

It seems that the only absolutely universal topic of conversation is the weather, which is totally gender neutral. Cute or funny things pets do is a close runner-up, among 'safe' talking topics to either men or women. Food is usually also reliably neutral as a conversation topic.

Men still have a tendency to talk to each other mostly about team sports, cars, hunting, extreme sports, electronics, racing and other auto sports, and, of course, more sports (however, never do these sports include figure skating). These are the safe, familiar topics of 'guy talk.'

They know stats and names of players and all of the scores and who just got traded to what other team or league and tend to speak in a sort of secret code when talking among themselves about their favorite teams or players.

The same is true when talking about cars, car motors or car racing, or anything that involves internal combustion, speed, weapons, electronics or competition.

Men's conversations with other men generally stay on a very topical or cause-effect or problem-solution level. Most men prefer to seek and share information on a need-to-know basis.

This is true of almost all their conversations, no matter who they are talking with.

That topic is always something tangible – a team, a player, an object, a goal, a touchdown, the size of the screen, the speed of anything, the profit margin, the ROI, the "bottom line," who won, who lost...

Even when they do (rarely) talk about more personal subjects such as relationships or personal problems, the topic is only talked about briefly and generally down-played so as not to appear personal. And (does this surprise you, really?) even when they have feelings or emotions about that topic, when talking they are STILL going to fall back on their comfort zone of cause-effect or problem-solution.

Men will often touch on an issue and then make a joke of it as if the subject isn't important. That's not the truth – it is just that it makes them so uncomfortable that the joke or off-hand comment takes the pressure off. It saves embarrassment.

If it's a group of men and a serious topic (such as getting married) the talk can sound like a wall-to-wall joke-athon rather than a conversation. Not that it's funny (and to women overhearing this, it might be offensive) but just that this is guys, being guys, nervous about a Big Life Topic.

It doesn't mean they don't like the idea of marriage, fear commitment, don't want to be married to you – just that their comfort meter is way, WAY over in the red zone.

To a woman who isn't interested in sports or cars or the typical topics of men's conversations, all she can hear is a foreign language that makes no sense to her.

She can also be appalled if she accidently hears two or more men talking about a personal problem and making light of it or joking about it.

If women did this, it would mean something quite different.

When have you ever heard women discussing the technical features of, for example, one stand-mixer over another, or one vacuum cleaner versus the competitor's model? They're just machines, they all do the job (more or less) and when they wear out, you go out and buy another one.

But men can be endlessly fascinated by the merits of one machine over another. They'll stand there in the store, comparing the speed or suction power or amps or volts or whatever endlessly unless you put an end to it.

As a woman, if you were to hear another woman state a personal problem that clearly troubles her ("we might have to find a care home for my grandmother," for example, or "my son says he hates school"), and then make a joke about it, or say she was comparison shopping for a solution, consider how you'd react.

You'd be looking for the subtext, the body language, the facial expressions – is she bitter? Sarcastic? Resigned? Should you hug her, offer help, advice?

When a man does this, what you should do is none of the above. You should immediately change the subject because he's finished with it, at least right now. This is him indicating to you that you've gone way beyond his comfort level (difficult subject) or he hasn't had enough thinking time to be ready to discuss it.

You could acknowledge this, with respect, and request a time in the future to continue the conversation. Something like, "I understand you don't want to talk more about this now, but we need to work through this/resolve this issue/come to some sort of decision. How about if we go for a drive out in the country this weekend, maybe stop at that little place with the patio for lunch – and talk about it then. Do you think this will give you time to think it over first?"

I've found that when you get away from your phone (just turn it off), laptop, chores to do at home and all the distractions – kids, dogs, noisy neighbours, other needs of relatives, your boss, your customers, whatever is in your life – and just concentrate on the conversation, it helps both people focus.

Driving time is good…or a relaxed meal together that's served by someone else, or even a walk in the evening or going for a paddle on the lake. Anything that gets you both away from distractions and doing something together. (Does this sound like a date? There's no rule that says committed couples can't continue enjoying times alone together.)

While driving (or rowing or paddling or hiking or any number of other activities) there's no requirement for eye contact or body language. For most men, this can take some of the difficulty out of a difficult conversation, or one on a touchy topic. Most women want body language, for the additional information it provides in a conversation. But here's something to know about most men: when the topic is important to them, or difficult, more information might just be information overload, causing them to shut down like an overloaded circuit blows a fuse.

How Women Talk, What Men Hear

Many women have interests that are quite different from the interests of men. For those of us who weren't interested in team sports in school, some of those 'team spirit' skills might be undeveloped.

Traditionally, women's interests focused on home, relationships, children, style and fashion, cooking and caring for pets, younger children or whoever needed caring for at the moment.

While many women still love to talk about these topics, today we also talk more about plans and aspirations in work or career, hobbies, volunteering and leisure activities than men tend to do.

Women tend to be the same person, all the time.

If a woman is willing to talk about a personal problem with one person, she may also be willing to mention it when around other people. Most women have been taught to talk about feelings and emotions and are not embarrassed to do so because it just feels 'right.' It's just what we've done, all our lives. (Maybe too much).

As women, you could say we have a rich vocabulary about human feelings and emotions – like 20 words for snow that certain peoples of the North are said to have for what most of us simply refer to as "snow," regardless of if it is heavy, light, wet, dry, deep, melting, falling, etc.

Most men (even the most sensitive and 'in-touch' of men) lack this rich vocabulary of the emotions that most women are fluent in (and mostly take for granted that we are fluent in).

If women are appalled when they hear men make light of a personal problem, men are equally appalled to hear women openly talking about feelings, personal problems and even their bodies with other women.

What Each Gender Truly Values in a Conversation

One big difference, briefly mentioned above, is that men will tend to talk very differently around other men than they will if a woman is present. They have a third way of expressing themselves if alone with a woman. Men tend to be very aware that they 'put on' one version of themselves at work, another with male friends and a third with family members and at home.

Some men will frequently swear or use other 'bad language' when around other men, but not when there are women present. They will also be more able and willing to talk about personal issues when alone with a woman who they love and trust.

This is important when contrasting the conversational styles of men and women.

Men easily and automatically switch communication styles to fit the audience and situation; women usually must learn to do this.

Before I understood this, I once became so frustrated and angry with a man I was dating that I accused him of being Mr. Plastic because, in my mind, he was 'real' with me but being a fake version of himself with other people. This particularly annoyed me when he was Mr. Easygoing with his abusive boss, a person I loathed (as did most of his co-workers). What I failed to see was that my boyfriend was brilliantly managing his boss.

To me the issue was crystal clear. I wanted to know which person he truly was – the person he was when we were alone together, or the person he was with his awful boss.

He was completely baffled by my reaction and no amount of discussion changed this.

I thought he should move on to a position with a more intelligent and supportive manager so he could continue to grow in his career.

He was astounded, saying he liked his job and the company and the boss "wasn't that bad."

Playing to the audience is completely different than the way most women communicate unless it's a speech or presentation, not a conversation.

Women have more of a tendency to have one basic style of communication with a few subtle variations.

It's no wonder that this is very confusing for women to comprehend and to understand which style of communication to expect at any given time.

Men do value their conversations with women and enjoy some of these topics women value, but men tend to only enjoy those topics in what most women would view as small doses.

Men, like anyone else, value being heard, understood and cared about; the biggest difference being that the conversation is best appreciated if it is generally short and then more comfortable topics are introduced.

Many women don't understand why the conversation seemed to be going so well and then abruptly the topic was changed. They believe they may have said something wrong because they don't realize that it was simply time to go on to something else, as far as the man was concerned.

Another tip: Men see conversation as a straight line, from A to B to C etc. A conversation has a purpose and a goal. To men, this is logical, orderly and just makes sense.

To women, conversation is free-ranging, and what men complain is "scattered" or "all over the place." If you drew a picture of a conversation women are having, it would be an ever-expanding mind-map.

If you drew a picture of an ideal conversation from the male perspective, it would likely look more like a clean, simple formula that you could plot on a straight-line graph, something like this:

Fact A + Fact B + Fact C = Result D

What is Involved in a Good Conversation?

When two people are involved in a conversation, what is it they are trying to accomplish? What's the purpose of the conversation?

This may seem like an odd question. Women usually don't need any 'purpose' for casual conversations – the purpose, if there is one, is primarily enjoyment and, possibly, information-sharing.

A conversation can be about business, a friendly get together to see how each has been since the last time they met, a casual meeting among friends or a getting-to know-each-other-and-maybe-something will-grow-from-this conversation or even I-like-this-person-a-lot-and-want-to-know-more conversation.

If a woman is thinking of starting a relationship with the man she is talking to, obviously, she is looking for different signals from him than a business or casual conversation would elicit.

So, here is how a woman might think of that conversation and rate its 'quality' as a good talk:

- Does the man make eye contact and appear to be really listening?
- Does he encourage me to say more?
- Does he ask questions that keep the conversation going?

- Does he appear interested in what I have to say?
- Does the conversation feel like it is flowing naturally?
- Does he seem engaged in the topic, and in being here, now, with me?

If these are some of the signals a woman is receiving from the man she is talking to, the conversation is being perceived by both parties as meaningful.

In other words, they're both having a Quality Conversation.

BUT...

- Does he cut her off in mid-sentence to supply his own ideas?
- Do his eyes keep flicking away while she is speaking?
- Does he take a cell phone call, or text while only 'half' listening, or check his watch?
- Does he change the subject frequently?
- Does he appear impatient or restless?

If these are the signals he is sending, he is probably either not interested in the conversation or it has stayed on one subject beyond the time he believes it should have ended.

Many times, I've felt there is LOTS more to say about something when the man is signaling he's done (for now) with that topic.

The only thing for a smart woman to do is state the need – as in, "We have a problem to solve together," and ASK when he would be prepared to talk about it and work out a solution together.

Remember that women tend to remain on one subject longer than men do. He may not be bored with you; it may be the subject matter that's the problem.

If the conversation has been somewhat personal or intense, this is when it's important to be able to smoothly change the subject to something a little less intense and a bit more topical.

Men are less likely to be interested in exploring all the 'might happen' possibilities of a topic; most of them prefer solid facts to ever having to consider the 'what ifs.' Most men have little patience with the 'what ifs?' of a topic or problem, even when their jobs require them to consider these as a part of risk management.

If the man appears to regain focus after the subject has been changed, the woman can be certain that she still has his attention.

If not, it could simply be he has a problem to solve, someplace else to be, or he isn't ready to talk about this issue yet.

He could be overtired, feeling ill, worried about an upcoming event (such as tax season) …

It is not useful to speculate on 'why' he doesn't want to talk about something. It could be that there are some issues that are just off limits, even in the closest and most loving relationships. You aren't the same person – two hearts beating as one is romance, not real life. In any marriage (or committed long term relationship) there are really three 'people' – there's you, him and the overlapping part in the middle is the marriage.

Remember, to him, talking about something isn't taking action, and for most men action is the comfort zone because taking action is how you solve problems.

He wants to know what the problem is, consider (quickly) the few best options, pick one, and move on it. Then rinse and repeat.

How Does Talking & Listening Relate to Respect & Caring?

When a man opens up and talks to a woman about very personal topics and is willing to talk about feelings and beliefs, he's telling the woman that he trusts her enough to tell her things that few others know.

It makes him vulnerable.

She is being given information that could eventually be used against him by allowing others to find out about his feelings.

When a man is willing to share this information, he needs acceptance and understanding and to be able to stop the conversation when he becomes uncomfortable or feels he has revealed enough for one time.

If he is pushed or encouraged to share more than he is willing to at that moment, he may become resentful or distrustful of the woman's motives.

Opening up about emotions isn't comfortable territory for him. There's really nothing to gain from pushing a man to share his feelings with you. Allow him his space but let him also know he is being heard and accepted for who he is.

When you hear women say "I keep trying to get him to tell me how he's REALLY feeling, but he just won't…" you know that what she is really doing is pushing her man away.

Don't make this mistake. If and when he reveals something deeply personal, honor this.

Then change the topic to something more comfortable for him.

Should I Pretend to Be Interested?

Developing interests in some of the things that are important to him also signals to him that you care enough to become involved in his interests.

Don't try to become an expert on all his interests or leave all of your own interests behind. Men are just as good at spotting false interest (or any other type of falsehood) as women are.

Genuine interest is seductive.

Seeing someone passionately interested in something and growing as they learn about it and become more skilled in it is powerfully attractive.

However, if that passionately-interested person can think and talk of nothing else, soon it will bore everyone around them.

We are all attracted to passion that takes action.

Most men are entirely capable of understanding passion for sports, or in business; expressing passion towards people is trickier for them.

Develop some knowledge and understanding in one or two of his hobbies or favourite activities so that you can carry on conversations about the subjects and understand when he is explaining these to you.

For example, you could offer to be a cheerful companion to the next basketball/baseball/hockey game, or volunteer in some capacity at a team event if he's one of the players.

If you hate it, don't try to get involved in it; he will quickly figure out that you are not being genuine and resent it.

Find something that you can share with him that you can both enjoy (no, it doesn't have to be football or soccer or hockey – but it has to be something you can have in common).

What interests do you have that he might also enjoy (maybe on a more casual level)?

Fortunately, in today's culture, many men and women do share many of the same interests. Many women and men are both health-conscious and enjoy working out and cycling.

Many also enjoy the same sports or learning a 'new' sport together such as orienteering or joining a bowling league or taking golf lessons or learning to scuba dive together (then having the fun of a dive vacation).

There are subjects, activities and hobbies that both men and women can equally enjoy. When any relationship or friendship is developing, finding common pastimes is a wonderful way to get to know and appreciate each other. Best of all, it gives you something to talk about.

Chapter Four

Step 2. Recognize The Conversation Killers

Here are the things that both men and women find annoying in conversation. They may not be total annihilation to the conversation you're having with a man, but why would you risk it?

Interrupting

What interrupting really says is:

- I don't care what you are about to say – what I have to say is more important
- You are taking too long to say what you want to say – I am impatient, anxious,

stressed. I don't have time for you to get to what you were going to say

- My need to be heard is more important than your need to speak

- You must pay attention to me

- You don't matter; I do.

Nagging

One of the important guidelines that I learned in journalism class that I still use to this day is, "Tell them what you're going to tell them, tell them, then tell them what you told them." It's known as the "Rule of Three."

Telling them three times works well in a lot of situations including presentations or a book, like this one.

1. Tell them what to expect – give a short overview of the topic, or a teaser to get them interested

2. Cover the topic in an orderly way, from Cause to Effect or Problem to Best Solution or chronologically.

3. Briefly recap what you told them.

When you tell people something more than three times, they start to resent it.

Back when everyone listened to music on record players, nagging used to be referred to as "sounding like a broken record," that is, stuck in one spot, playing the same few bars of music over and over.

If you have told someone something three times and you have not received a reply, chances are that person isn't going to reply or do whatever it is you have requested.

And, right now, they're sick of the broken record.

If that person has agreed to a request and then either not acted or appears to have forgotten, ask yourself how many times you have made the request. If you've already said it three times, you may need to say it again, but keep in mind that the person really does know that you have said it.

The real question may become why he isn't responding when he knows what you want.

If it's a petty task (put out the recycling bin; take the car in for an oil change, take the dog to the vet) make the reminder once, but leave it up to him about when he'll do it.

If it's about something bigger (get your passport renewed so we can go away this winter; we need a bigger home) you could ask if he has the information and make a 'date' to talk about it.

Then, clear distractions, and have a focused, problem-solving conversation based on fact (here's the checklist of everything we have to do to go away this winter or why we need to move, where to, steps to take).

The Silent Treatment

It's one thing to agree to come back to a topic when emotions are high or one person has just had enough, for now.

It's another to stomp off, sulk, or subject your partner to the silent treatment until you get what you want, such as an apology.

The first choice is negotiated between two adults; the second is using a behavior you may have learned as a child to manipulate (control, punish) the other person.

The first strengthens the bond between you; the second weakens it.

Here's another time when you might be using the Silent Treatment as far as he is concerned.

Imagine that you've had an upsetting experience. This isn't the usual everyday sort of annoyance like being cut off by another driver or stuck in a slow line at the check-out. This is something major such as betrayal by someone you thought was a friend. Or having proof that someone you trusted is stealing from you.

Naturally, you're upset. Preoccupied. Not your usual self.

"What's the matter?" your boyfriend or partner says. In his mind, very obviously, something isn't right. He needs to find out what and fix it so you can go back to being your usual self and you both can enjoy the evening together.

"Nothing," you say, hoping he'll just drop it. "I'm just tired...have a headache...it's that time of month..." or whatever excuse you choose to use.

But he doesn't just drop it because in his world, Happy Wife, Happy Life is the rule that applies here. He'd be a Jerk if he ignored you being unhappy and did nothing. Therefore, it's his job to get you back to happy, which means fixing your problem.

But you aren't happy.

You don't want to talk about it, not yet because you haven't quite taken it in. It's big, it's complex, you have to come at it from several angles, consider the reasons it happened, the consequences, what to do next…you don't want a 'fix' because there isn't one.

You want to think it through, talk about it (eventually) with people who have an emotional understanding of this situation, and that might be your man; or maybe not.

It might be a Girlfriend topic.

It depends on how he listens. With empathy? With compassion for how you're feeling? Not leaping in with solutions?

Some men can be good at these skills, or even exceptionally good. In the real world, few are unless they've been specifically taught AND are motivated to learn.

Think about this for a moment: for him, if he doesn't have these skills, doesn't even recognize them as skills, it could be about as difficult as you suddenly deciding that you're going to become fluent in Ancient Greek. You're willing to do this because he would feel better if you two sometimes communicated in that language.

To him, the emotional language of women, the one we've had years (and more likely decades) of experience communicating with, might be as foreign as the world's most obscure language would be to you.

So what to do when you've had a shattering experience, he asks what's wrong, you're tempted to brush him off with the "nothing" lie...?

Instead, why not say, "Something happened today (or I've learned something) that I will tell you about, but not yet. I just need time to think about it before I'm ready. It's new information I need to process." And change the subject. Then try, as much as you can to enjoy the evening with him.

Processing new information – that will sound reasonable, even logical, to him.

It's better than leaving him feeling rejected, out in the cold, unable to help you.

The fact is, he is helping you by giving your active brain a bit of a time out while in the background it begins to work through what you need to do next which, logically, is get you back in control of your life.

Assuming Can Lead to Trouble

This is as bad on the Conversation Quality meter as interrupting.

If someone is speaking, allow that person to finish their thought.

Even if you believe you understand what is being said, people feel frustrated when they are interrupted and really annoyed when you leap ahead of them with that thought.

Repeating Yourself

Remember the "Rule of Three." Once you have said something three times, you have exhausted its usefulness and you are back to either nagging or becoming boring.

Women (talking among ourselves) usually have a much higher tolerance for circling back, looking at things from (yet another) angle and analyzing a given situation in minute detail.

To men (immune to the subtleties) this is just same old all over again.

IS This The Right Place, The Right Time?

This is sometimes an easy mistake for women to make because we are not always used to the way men categorize conversations.

Men tend to discuss topical subjects in public places or with more than one person present and more personal subjects in private settings.

If you would like to discuss a private or personal matter, choose a quiet time and place where it will only be the two of you.

Even if it doesn't seem all that private or personal to YOU, it might be for him. Err on the conservative side – keep it private.

I have found it helpful to give a man 'thinking it through' time before a serious topic conversation, and requesting a 'date' to do this after giving a very brief outline of what we will be talking about.

And NEVER start with "We need to talk." That's a red flag to men, giving them the overpowering urge to run for the exits, probably because it sounds too much like an authority figure (parent, teacher, the principal) demanding better behavior from a child.

Not only is talking 'down' to someone, or talking to them as if they are a very young child disrespectful, it will cause them to distrust you and become (depending on the person and situation) annoyed, angry, resentful, possibly even vengeful.

Talk as equals, because you are. You are both reasonable, intelligent, thoughtful adults, aren't you? So, talk to him that way.

Something like this works better:

"We're going away this winter for a dive vacation, but we need to make reservations soon to take advantage of the seat sales. There are plenty of options, but I've done some reading and I think we'd both really like either Costa Rica or Belize the best. Would you have a look at these brochures (or go to these websites) and let's pick one. Would talking about it at dinner on Friday give you enough time to decide which one you'd like the best? I like them all/I really prefer Resort X, would you like to go there?"

Here's why this works:

Start with what is already a Given (you're going on a vacation) so then you need to move this plan forward to The Next Step – Supporting Facts – Why there is Time Urgency – When To Resolve It And Reach A Sensible Decision and Make A Plan.

OF all of this, the FACTS are most important to him. So stress those. Where has the clearest water, the best reviews online, the best dive weather etc. etc.?

Does this sound just like problem-to-solution to you?

It's similar to what every journalism student learns first about what MUST be in the story (because that's what the audience wants to know):

WHO – WHAT – WHERE – WHEN – WHY and maybe, HOW.

It all has to be there but doesn't have to be in that exact order.

It does have to be specific. Facts. Quotes. Numbers.

It must be verified – not just someone's opinion, unless quoted as just someone's opinion (they better be a person with credibility if so).

Do your homework before this conversation if you want a happy result.

There needs to be a deadline, a problem to be solved, and a BIG benefit when it is solved.

That's what makes sense to men and to women, too, when we understand it and use it skillfully. We get what we both want (that wonderful vacation), you get what you want (his involvement) and he gets what he wants (you happy, his chance to relax).

While I've given a personal example, this method works just as well on the job, with your Dad, or any man you want to communicate effectively with and also with male children old enough to reason with.

And it works well for any decision that needs to be made, or any situation in which you feel you are 'stuck' and not getting anywhere.

What Were We Just Talking About...?

Some people will begin to ramble because of nervousness and not even realize they are doing it.

Men tend to be more comfortable with silence than most women. Silence just about never happens amongst a group of women.

Long pauses, or not talking does not signal to a man that something is wrong.

Men also prefer the 'straight line' conversation, from point A to B with no side-trips.

There is also the comfortable silence when nothing really needs to be said right now.

Issuing Ultimatums, And Where That Gets You

No one likes an ultimatum.

It can feel like a threat Or bullying.

It is disrespectful and manipulative. A display of power.

And it's unkind.

Sometimes – very rarely – it is your last option.

If you are ready to issue an ultimatum, you need to be ready to follow through on whatever the threat is (there always is a threat in there).

If you are ready to end a relationship for some real reason unless he does something specific (propose, for example, or stop gambling), then state that very clearly and be ready to pack your bags, or watch him leave.

If you don't intend on doing something as drastic as you are threatening, don't say you will.

Ultimatums are a final measure and if there's any way to correct a problem without using one, that's what you must do.

The reason is that ultimatums – even when he stays, or you do – will damage your relationship, long term. They are difficult to recover from because they are a breach of trust. Ultimatums are a power play. They're the way you treat a hostage, not a friend or a lover.

The Art – And Goal – Of Talking To Men

Are you rambling again? Are you babbling?

No, just talking normally… but maybe that's not what he's hearing.

Are you speaking to hear your own voice because the silence is uncomfortable?

Are you talking your way around the topic, as you would with women friends or your mother?

Just thinking out loud?

Seeking attention?

Anxious?

More aware of your own need at the moment than his?

Are you speaking to cover up a problem? Or divert attention from a more difficult topic?

If there is a problem to address, then talk about it or set up an appropriate time when the two of you can talk about it.

If you are talking needlessly, ask yourself why. You will likely find a problem hidden away that you are worried about. Maybe you need to think it through before talking about it.

Are You Bonding, Or Is It Just Too Much Small Talk?

To women, LOTS of talk is getting to know each other, getting closer, enjoying each other's company. It's fun.

Most men wouldn't see it that way.

Talking about the weather, where you're going on vacation, your sister just had a baby... all small talk, as far as men are concerned.

Remember, men and women do have some similar interests and they also have some diverse interests.

Always keep in mind who you are talking to and what that person may or may not be interested in. This is a good rule for any conversation.

Don't assume, based on gender, what subjects are appropriate and which are not. There are ways to check and see if the subject matter is acceptable or not; try one or two sentences about a subject and then pause and check the person's response.

If you believe you have that person's interest, then continue. If it appears that it isn't a topic the person is interested in, move on to something else.

The Blame Game

It's all his fault – all he ever wants to do is argue. Or avoid "real issues" and go out with the guys.

Or it's all because you had a difficult childhood – or he did.

Or because of all the stress at work.

Or his awful job, the long hours you or he work, the beast of a boss, that vampire co-worker…

There's no end to what, or who else, you could blame when life isn't what you want it to be and you aren't happy.

Truly getting to that happier place (rather than just staying in the blame and complain trap) means you must work with your man as a team to tackle the core problem or problems. That core problem might mean some difficult changes. But it could also mean you grow closer as, together, you build that better life.

Whining, Complaining, Feeling Sorry for Yourself, Negativity

Do you know people who are always complaining or whose problems are always worse than yours?

Do you have friends who call and you dread picking up the phone because they are going to bring you down, emotionally?

Do you have a colleague or relative whose life seems to be in a constant state of crisis?

Don't be one of these people.

It can be a bad habit to fall into, always complaining, or always finding fault. It can also be difficult to recognize that you do this. A close and loving friend may be able to alert you, if you have one of these conversational bad habits.

They won't want to tell you this 'bad' news. If they do, thank them sincerely. Then you need to do some work to uncover the underlying reasons you've fallen into a poor-me rut. It could be anxiety, or a problem with confidence or self-esteem, or just not having enough in your life to be proud of.

If so, it is in your power to change this.

If this is the case, friends can be supportive, but it's better to turn to a professional counselor to work through the problem and find the right way to help yourself be happier and emotionally healthier.

It's worth the investment, because it will pay off in benefits with your relationships with everyone in your life, beginning with yourself.

Talking positive leads to thinking positive, and that makes for a happier life.

Research backs this up. When psychologist John Mordechai Gottman looked into what determines whether a marriage endures or fails, he discovered the single most important factor or predictor of either success or failure is how often a couple give each other positive messages. He determined that the optimal ratio is five positive comments for every negative one. He published his findings in *The Relationship Between Marital Processes and Marital Outcomes* in 2009.

WAY Too Much Emotion -- Angry Outbursts, Road Rage, Running Away

Emotions are good.

Sometimes, when, where and how we express emotions are not so good.

If you have emotional outbursts, make scenes or tend to leave a room in anger or tears, you may have a problem starting a relationship or keeping a healthy one going.

Outbursts that occur on a regular basis may signal that you have problems expressing your emotions in a healthy, positive way.

It could be that you are overly sensitive, what some people call being "thin-skinned," and may need to be aware of that and take steps to build up your inner strength and resiliency.

It could be you are overreacting to situations, or you are using your emotions as a tool to manipulate others.

It may be things that happened in your past are still causing you trouble now and need to be explored.

Whatever the cause, emotional outbursts are difficult for most people to comfortably deal with. They find it confusing and embarrassing. If the outbursts are used to manipulate, they will quickly lose their effectiveness.

If you feel like you cannot control these outbursts, please see a counselor or therapist. You are obviously having problems that should be addressed by someone who can help you release yourself from the grip of these stormy emotions to feel happier and more in control.

Major Disconnect: When all You Want is Your Feelings Validated, But He Wants to Fix the Problem

Sometimes we just need to cry or rant and rave and that is all that we really want to do because we must get those negative feelings out and have someone just listen.

Or we need to work our way through a problem or issue out loud. For some of us, that's part of the process, hearing ourselves think.

We don't want someone else to supply The Answer or The Solution, we just want to be heard, validated, and most of all, understood.

If you do this around someone who always wants to fix and repair things, he may not understand that you just need to talk. Make it a point to let him know exactly what you need from him. Don't make him guess or assume he 'should know,' because, after all, if he loves you he would just automatically know what you want/need/think. No, he doesn't.

If you just need someone to listen, plainly explain that to him, not in a 'you're so dumb' tone of voice but as a reasonable request.

If you need to bounce ideas off him and get his ideas and input, let him know that's what you need.

If he starts to take over and make plans to deal with the problem or situation on his own, complete with ready-made solutions that start with "You should…" or "You have to…" then you need to be able to tell him that it isn't his job to do this.

There are many situations where a man will want to take your problems into his own hands. That isn't just a nice gesture; it's him being a man.

He has an actual, primal, Mind-and-Gut NEED to step in, take over, solve the problem, as he sees it.

The emotions surrounding that problem are not relevant.

The people needs might be minor, or not relevant – simply, in his opinion, distractions.

It's a problem, that problem is likely in some way mechanical, it can be fixed. By him.

It is so critical to understand this about men. They don't just want or like to 'fix' things, their brains are hard-wired to fix things.

If you have younger brothers, or sons, you will recognize that this shows up early in a boy's life.

"Make It Right," as Mike Holmes says of the botched home renos he fixes (thereby rescuing the families that are cowboy-reno victims) on his series of home improvement TV shows. Everybody hugs at the end of these shows, and Mike the Man beams his pleasure. But the REAL pleasure was he is reconfirmed in his manliness because he fixed the problems (shelter) not because he wanted applause for being a nice guy.

Do you see the hero cape, along with the power tools? This ISN'T posturing. It's being fully alive, as a man.

Every man can relate...

To them, an unresolved situation needs to be fixed.

All he wants to do is protect you and make you happy.

Chivalry isn't dead; men still have the instinct and the NEED to protect the people they love (and, depending on the individual man, this could extend to everyone they know and even complete strangers).

Imagine there is a problem. It's been there for a while. You're frustrated. He, it seems, is ignoring this problem.

If you were to step in to solve this problem for him (or for you both), would that be a good idea?

If he becomes angry or threatened and thinks you are in danger his testosterone is going to increase and he is going to want to become aggressive and run out and slay a few dragons.

It's as simple as that. It can take some quick talking to avert a problem when that happens because all he wants to do is protect you and 'make' you happy.

Often that's good. Sometimes it totally misses the point because you just want a sounding board. You just want to vent. You just want to cry. You just want him to put his arms around you and assure you that things are going to work out somehow.

Something that happened to my sister really touches on this idea. She was rushing around one morning, already running late, trying to get the kids in the car and it was her turn to do the school run, so she had a couple of other kids to pick up. And it was freezing out.

Then she found out the car was dead. Turned the key and – nothing.

Her husband had already left for work.

She debated calling him, but instead, she called one of the other mothers.

"Wow," the woman said. "How are you going to get the kids to school? Let me call Terri (the other mother whose child is in their carpool for the school run)."

In just a moment, Terri called. "Hold on," she said. "I'll be there in 10." And she was, to get all the kids to school, and on the way drop my sister off at the bus stop, so my Sis got to work only half an hour late.

Meanwhile, she called her husband. "Did you try just waiting a few minutes and trying again?" he asked. "Are you sure you didn't flood the engine…? OK, well did you call the Auto Club to come give you a jump?"

See the difference here? To women, it was all about the taking-care-of-people nurturing issue. Kids need to get safely to school. Woman friend needs to get to her job.

But to my brother-in-law, using his man-communication system, the thought process was 'she's having a problem with the car' and he leapt into fix-it mode, something like this: Car Doesn't Work. Wife Needs Car. Fix Car.

Both genders were fixing problems. It's just that the problems they were fixing – people problem or machine problem – were different.

Same result though – people got to where they needed to be. Car (later, not sooner) got fixed.

Crying

I once had an unhappily single female colleague who cried very easily when she was confused, when she was upset, when she was frustrated by a new task, when she was confronted by any sort of opposition, when she was challenged, when she was feeling overworked, when she couldn't get organized, when she was reminded about the tasks she didn't do by her boss because she was always so disorganized ...all the time, it seemed.

At work, she didn't rush off to the Women's Room to do this crying. She just burst into tears.

All of us who had to work with her appreciated her skills in the core responsibilities of her job. In some of these, she was very skilled and talented. But overall we found it hard to work with her. It was just annoying to have to deal with all this emotion, especially for our boss, who was an understanding, decent, good man who had a department to run efficiently.

In our workplace, the practice was to 'fix' people. Rarely was anyone ever laid off or fired.

But this colleague of ours did not see that she had a problem – only that people kept "picking on" her, as she put it. Same thing had happened on the jobs she used to have. It was like people were always ganging up on her. Or at least that's what she thought.

Crying is something men rarely do, and even more rarely do they do it in front of others. If they do, it embarrasses and confuses them.

It also embarrasses and confuses them when other people cry.

A study published in *Science Magazine* in 2011 has shown that tears don't just cause a man to be uncomfortable, they set off chemical changes in his body and brain that make him distinctly uncomfortable.

The astonishing conclusion of this study is that women's tears cause a man to produce less testosterone.

To put it another way, tears make him less manly. And this is intolerably uncomfortable.

Believe it or not, it isn't the sight of the tears; it is the smell that turns men off, Dr. Naom Sobel and his colleagues at Weizmann Institute of Science in Israel concluded.

It seems a woman's emotional tears emit an odor that causes men to react when it lowers testosterone levels.

Men will often have no idea why they are reacting to the woman's tears, but they distinctly don't like the feelings those tears produce, and now we know why.

This is not to say you can never, ever cry in front of a man. Just recognize that crying is an emotional release he (likely) can't handle. It's NOT a way to communicate with him.

Other Communication Mistakes & What to Do Instead

Lack of Confidence

I have just touched on the role confidence plays in talking and listening effectively. Having a strong sense of self is important, but let's just take a moment to consider it and how it relates to talking to men and listening to men.

Confidence is attractive, in and to anyone.

Think of the most attractive man and the most attractive woman you either know or know of (perhaps they are a celebrity).

Subtract confidence from the mix. Take away the eye contact, the good posture, the easy smile, the friendly way they have when talking to anyone and what do you have?

Pretty or handsome; perhaps. But not 'popular' (back in school), and not likely to be liked and respected (successful) as an adult. Or considered attractive, in the basic sense of that word – they attract people.

If you want to be more attractive to everyone, including men, check your confidence. It can get you way more than anything you could buy at the mall.

Stop Apologizing

Have you known a person who is constantly apologizing, or putting themselves down?

Is it just a bad habit? Is it lack of confidence? Is it something else?

Could be any of these, but unless you are close to that person, you aren't likely to want to know them.

Or could this be you?

If so, suggestions elsewhere in this book can help you and it might be an area of your life that you could improve if you work with a life coach or a therapist.

Your Tone of Voice

Do you speak with confidence and authority?

For some women, that may mean consciously lowering your voice, when with men, or a mixed group of men and women, or for serious topics.

If you are a fan of the TV show *The Big Bang Theory*, you may have noticed that one of the women characters, Bernadette, always talks in a little-girl voice.

It's cute and funny on the show because the running gag is that she has more education, a much better job and makes more money than her husband. Clearly, she's in charge.

While this is fun to watch, in real life a grown woman who talks baby talk or in a babyish voice is treated like what she sounds like, a child.

A lowered voice carries authority and demonstrates confidence.

Cool Technique - The 'I-When-Please Do This' Message

When you begin a sentence with the word "I" instead of "You," you can frequently avoid sounding like you are accusing someone or something (and their ear hears "Oh-Oh. Time to tune out").

They need to hear the what and the when, specifically.

They also need to hear what you would prefer to happen instead, as a polite request.

So, here's a good I-When-Please Do This Message in action:

"I get worried when you are not here on time. When you are going to be later than just 10 minutes or so, could you text me or call, please?"

That's a lot easier to process than:

"You're late again," an accusation that can lead to, *"You're always so thoughtless,"* which is an over-generalization and an accusation, probably leading to another pointless, frustrating argument.

Don't fall into that "You always…you never," conversation trap. In relationships, absolutes are seldom true. The other person becomes defensive, there's an argument, hard feelings and nothing gets communicated.

What you could call a lose-lose situation.

Giving Feedback

When someone is talking to you, say back to that person what you just heard to make sure you understood what is being said.

Don't assume you understand without checking. What you heard may not be what he thought he said.

Don't Issue Orders

Asking pleasantly can accomplish so much more (this is why no one likes the drill sergeant).

Explain why you are asking.

"Pick me up at noon," is a bit abrupt.

This works better:

"Please pick me up at noon; I have an appointment at 12:15, so that should be enough time to get there, don't you think?" is clear and not an order.

Then confirm: "OK, great, see you at noon. Thanks!"

The Pause With Possibilities

Take just half a second to respond. It tells the other person that you're really listening and waiting until he or she is finished talking before you reply.

Think of taking a pause or continuing a conversation in the future as a way to ease up and let some air into the conversation and your relationship.

The Difference Between Feelings & Thoughts

Feelings are emotions: Happy, sad, glad, angry, surprised, annoyed, thrilled...

If someone asks you how you are feeling and you can answer in one word that is most likely a feeling.

If the answer takes several words, you are probably replying with a thought or a belief.

Thoughts might just be beliefs, true or false. Use the word "believe" instead of "think" or "feel" and if it works, it probably is a belief and you need to check and make sure your belief is correct.

It could be the man you are talking to believes something quite different.

If so, that could depend on his role in your life, which is what we're going to look more closely at next, in Step 3.

Chapter Five

Step 3. Who HE Is Matters

Do you talk to your brother, your Dad, your colleague, boss and your boyfriend or husband in (more or less) the same way, same tone of voice, using the same conversation habits (if not precisely the same topics)?

If so, write this on down and post it where you will see it often.

How You relate to Him Depends On the Role He Plays in Your Life

He's not Daddy, and you're no longer his little girl. No whining, no cajoling, no baby talk.

He's not an authority figure – he's not your teacher, boss, mentor or leader. You don't 'report' to him. Or ask for an allowance. Or need permission to be who you are.

He's not your child, dependent on you for nurturing, the necessities of life and loving protection and guidance to adulthood (and beyond). You're both adults. As such, you are each responsible for your own happiness.

He's not 'just' a friend. It's good if he's your friend, better if he's your best friend…but if you're living together or married, and even if you recognize there's a strong attraction, but there is no relationship yet…you've moved beyond friendship to a deeper level.

He's not a colleague. Or a casual acquaintance.

He's not a renovation project. You married him to love him as he is (just as he loves you for who you are), not to improve him. If either of you try to 'improve' the other person, you are in for years of frustration – that is, if your relationship lasts that long.

He is: Someone You're Very Attracted To

DO: It's always 'safe' to talk about the event you're both at, the venue, the meal, the weather...but that is less interesting than when you try to find some interests you have in common.

Ask questions about his hobbies, what he likes the most about his work, his favourite vacation destination and why, his favourite restaurant, what kind of music he likes and why or books or movies ...

Be careful to make these questions friendly and open-ended – not like a job interview.

DON'T: Don't ask very personal questions or offer information about yourself that he might find embarrassing, such as about your breakup with your most recent boyfriend. It's too early to do this.

Keep it light, positive, fun.

Listen as much as you talk.

Expect it to be brief (leave him wanting more time with you).

He is: Your Current Boyfriend Or Partner (Husband)

DO: Listen when he speaks. Allow him to express himself before you speak.

Be kind.

Treat him as you wish to be treated.

Be specific. Ask for what you need and want.

Understand his need to be your hero, to make you happy by solving all your problems, and that you are very possibly his only emotional outlet and support.

DON'T: Don't interrupt his conversation to refocus it on you.

Don't dump bad news or negative comments on him when you first get together after work or after being separated for several hours or days. Be positive and show it.

Give both of you a chance to unwind from the day – he may need a few minutes of 'alone time' to adjust, right after getting home, before talking to you.

Real Men Don't Show Their Emotions

This is about as true as saying Real Women don't ever change tires, handle the family finances skillfully, demonstrate leadership or have career ambitions.

Yet there are people who still think that using emotional language is somehow un-manly or unattractive in a 'real' man. There is, ironically, nothing logical about this belief.

And before you dismiss it as cave-man thinking, or say that as an intelligent and thoughtful woman you would never get involved with a man like that, consider this: it's a fairly common belief among even intelligent and thoughtful men that there is something 'undignified' and maybe even childish about expressing or validating emotions.

Beware the man with such limited emotional scope that the only emotion he knows how to express is anger. You aren't likely to be the woman who 'fixes' him or helps him see the error of his ways and broaden his communication skills. You might present the information, but only he can do what's required to take advantage of it.

Chapter Six

Step 4. Don't Make These Common Listening Mistakes!

Some of these mistakes have already been mentioned, so this section is a mix of new tips and review:

Assuming You Already Know What He Thinks or is About to Say

Never assume.

Allow him to complete his thought before you say anything. Women are used to talking over and around each other. Men aren't.

Ask questions to make sure the message received = message sent.

Leaping to Conclusions

You think it's already decided; he doesn't.

You're just seeking the rubber stamp approval, he needs more thinking time.

You're ready to move on; he isn't.

If you are not interested in getting any feedback or listening to any suggestions, tell him first.

Let him know you are not open to any suggestions; you have already made up your mind and are not willing to entertain any ideas but your own.

Also make sure that, if it all blows up in your face, you take all the responsibility.

Dominating the Conversation

Are you having a conversation or are you giving a speech?

If you value him as a person, allow him the opportunity to be involved in the conversation and listen to what he has to say.

Always Being on the Defensive -- It's Not My Fault

This is hard to deal with, whether it's a man or a woman.

It's difficult to carry on a conversation with someone who's overly sensitive, always looking for insults in what people say, always being defensive or always convinced people are out to get him or her.

Or perhaps that's you?

If people feel that talking to you is like tip-toeing on eggs, they will do anything to avoid you.

If you must get along with someone like this, my recommendation is that you keep things entirely fact-based.

If they become upset or defensive, immediately stop, say "We'll get back to this when you are feeling more yourself," and end the conversation.

Pretending to Listen, But You're A Million Miles Away

Ok, no woman would blame you if your child was in danger, if your wedding is next week, if you've got killer cramps or if there is some other MAJOR thing going on in your life, and you are having some difficulty focusing on the moment.

If that's true, admit it. Briefly. Then try to re-focus on here and now.

If what he's saying isn't important to you, then be honest and tell him.

If you're having trouble concentrating because you're ill or there is something in the area that is distracting, let him know.

You may need to move to a different location or have the conversation at another time.

Wrong Time, Wrong Place

Imagine you're in bed, you've just had a nice time, and suddenly he says one of these things:

We should get married. Say yes!

I've been thinking. We should move to Africa…or maybe Japan…

Why don't you quit your job and move in with me?

Why don't I quit my job and move in with you?

How would you react?

Plainly put, there is a time and a place for everything, or anything.

You will both be wasting time, effort and energy if you try to have a conversation at the wrong time or place.

Respect your needs and his enough to postpone or change locations. Or times.

If he doesn't understand this concept, use your "I" message to request a change.

Comparing Him, and/or His Communication Style, To Other People You've Known

Being compared to someone else is a bad idea. He doesn't want to hear about your ex/former boyfriend or your Dad or, especially, how someone you know or used to know was so much better at feelings, listening, giving you support, etc. than he is.

A more positive way is simply and honestly to ask for what you need.

Making It All About You

Do you think he's in a bad mood because of something you said or did? Could it be that his bad mood has nothing to do with you, he just had a bad day or some sort of set-back you don't know about yet? Why not simply ask him? Validate the feeling he's having – ask for what he needs (which might simply be a bit of quiet time).

Living The Dream

Some people are so consumed by Living The Dream life and thinking that their real life can't possibly measure up that they are constantly unhappy. This is true of the person who thinks the honeymoon phase of the relationship should never end, then is miserable when it does.

Or she believes she should have the type of marriage she imagines a certain celebrity enjoys or just like a "blissfully happy" couple she once knew.

Real relationships ebb and flow. There are better times, and there are problem times. No one gets the perfect relationship, because it doesn't exist and it's exhausting trying to create it.

Better to accept that he will never be perfect and neither will you. You'll never be exactly who and what he wants in every way. He'll never be Mr. Perfect.

He Should She Should

It's a mistake to get caught up in *shoulds*, that list of unwritten rules about your relationship that haven't been discussed but you still get upset or angry when he doesn't say or do your *should*.

Things like:

He should always remember to bring home flowers on your birthday and anniversary along with a wrapped gift.

You should always cook a big meal for Sunday dinner and invite the family over.

Since you have much better taste, he should gratefully accept and wear the clothing you buy for him and throw out those awful, unflattering clothes he bought.

He should want to spend more time with you.

You should spend more money. Or save more.

He should just know what you need when you're upset.

He should be a mind-reader because he loves you.

You should never be bored when you're together.

He should never be angry.

And this is the big one: If we're truly in love, it should all just come naturally. We shouldn't have to discuss things or argue about them. Our life (including our sex life) should always be fantastic. If not, we aren't in the right relationship with the right person.

Consider your *shoulds.*

Ask him what his *shoulds* are.

Can you substitute "Let's try…" for a should that you really want or he really wants (or you both do) and see if you can get it, working together? For example, the desire for flowers and a gift on a birthday or anniversary might just be about "Let's try to remember to make birthdays and anniversaries special."

Chapter Seven

Step 5. Reading His Signals

Let's consider all the information you can get even if you can't hear the words – or if they are spoken in a language you don`t understand.

Have you ever watched a conversation across a room, perhaps at a restaurant, or at a gathering – a wedding reception perhaps, or a trade show or charity event?

Or watched a TV show with the sound muted?

It`s amazing how much you can tell about what is being said when you can`t hear the words.

Add in the information body language and facial expressions reveal and you learn a lot more that 'just' what the person is saying in words.

Here's how to use this to your advantage when you're listening and when you're talking:

Eye Contact

Eye contact is critical in Western countries and those with a European heritage, such as Australia and South Africa.

In these cultures, avoiding eye contact is suspicious. We tend to think that people who don't make eye contact are possibly hiding something. Or perhaps they are lying.

In fact, very skilled liars can look right at you while spinning their fantasies.

But there aren't many highly skilled liars in the world, fortunately.

Eye contact is a cultural trait. We value it and expect it in Western cultures. This is quite different in some other cultures, as I discovered when I lived in South Korea. There, children are taught that eye contact isn't just challenging and aggressive, it is rude.

What we do in the Western world is look to the eyes as a window to the mind, heart and soul.

Making eye contact tells a person that you are interested in what is being said, that you are listening to the words and that you are not intimidated.

Nodding Agreement. Or Disagreement

Agreement is when you nod your head (up and down) and disagreement is when you frown, look away, and possibly nod your head (side to side). Again, this is cultural, in the Western world. In some cultures nodding means something quite different.

Impatience or Anger

There are many body language signals of impatience or anger:

- Tightening the jaw, clenching teeth, tightening fists
- Frowning

- Tapping a foot or fingers
- Not making eye contact; seeming to be distracted
- Increasing the physical distance between you

Arm-crossing and What it Means

If you sit or stand with your arms crossed in front of you, you are sending a message that you are closed to that person or feeling defensive.

Some people are often not even aware that they are doing this and others stand or sit that way most of the time.

The truth is the speaker is getting a signal from you that all is not well.

If you're talking to someone who does this, be fact-based, be brief and end the conversation quickly.

Sighing

Sighing is a sign of boredom, being tired or disgusted.

It is a sure signal to the person speaking that you are not listening or wish he would stop talking.

Stance

Stance refers to the way you are standing.

Is your stance conveying that you are listening? Yes, if:

- You're leaning toward the speaker rather than away from them. You are leaning in.

- Your arms are at your sides, hands open and relaxed, demonstrating that you are 'open' to what the speaker has to say

Angled Body

Here is something that men and women share. Standing with your body angled to his when talking, rather than face-to-face directly across from each other, is more 'comfortable' because it is experienced, by both genders, as less confrontational (unless you share an intimate relationship).

As a woman, if you don't want to be a 'threat' to a man you are talking to, angle your body (a one-quarter turn) to talk to him.

If your boyfriend or lover (or anyone) is sending signals that they are uncomfortable talking, it can help to sit side-by-side, rather than opposite each other.

The Power Of Touch

Women tend to take touch for granted.

Men don't.

Touch means I Like You. A man who really wants to know you better is going to look for opportunities to touch you.

The exception: in some cultures, (more so Europe than America), kissing (on the cheeks) is a greeting, even for complete strangers, and even among business contacts, rather than a firm handshake.

The pandemic has changed this to elbow-touching or other 'almost' touching gestures. Once this threat has been dealt with and we all feel safe again, I predict that handshaking and hugging will return as a greeting.

The Lean-in

When someone is speaking and you lean slightly toward that person, you convey that you are really listening and interested in what the person is saying.

You like what you're hearing; you want more.

In a dating situation, the lean-in means I Want to Know You Better.

Chapter Eight

Step 6. Where's This Going?

Conversation among women is usually something like a day on a river that meanders back and forth across a flood plain. It isn't planned, it just flows, as the sun comes out or goes behind the clouds, perhaps bringing rain before the sun returns. Everyone enjoys the journey, the constantly changing scenery, the many changes in direction.

To men, conversation is more of an event with a Beginning, a Middle, and an End. There's a definite destination and you take the direct path to get there.

When talking to men of any age, even very little boys, conversations are only worth paying attention to if they have a clear purpose and a goal, like get candy or permission to play computer games for another half hour before bed.

How 'planned up' do you need to be to talk to males, including men?

If you are:

- anxious about an upcoming event (or avoiding it)
- nervous about meeting someone for the first time
- have a big date planned with someone special
- facing someone to stand up for your rights
- there's a Big Ask involved – such as: Let's not go skiing this winter, I'd rather go to the beach
- you need buy-in, such as their support or help

Or you have any desired result in mind, you may want to give some thought to planning your conversation.

Any sensible woman would be likely to 'think ahead' in any of these circumstances.

What I recommend is that you do the same for most, maybe all conversations with men (or boys).

Trust me, they do, because it works for them. They get to the destination – or change tactics and try again.

A cultural thing. To boys, quitters are sissies. They'd rather do anything than be seen as a crier, a baby or a quitter.

It requires extra effort to plan before talking. To women, it may feel a bit contrived; not-quite-comfortable and unnatural. Even as if you are setting the stage for a given outcome which, of course, you are.

So, what do YOU get when you do this?

- You make a positive first impression
- You get 'buy-in,' that is, they want to support your initiative, vote for your candidate, help you reach your worthy goal etc.

- They want to see you again (they want to keep the conversation going)

You're planning a conversation, not a speech. The goals and planning for each are different.

When giving a speech, you are the only one who will be talking, so it's much more specific and you can plan each word if you choose to do so.

Not so with a conversation. You can plan the topics you hope to cover, you can plan on a possible outcome, but you cannot anticipate with 100% accuracy what the other person or people will say or what direction the conversation will move in. Chances are it will surprise you. New information, new directions, new possibilities for the future may emerge in a conversation.

How to Set Conversation Goals

It can help to organize your thoughts when you start out with pen and paper or laptop and write notes, listing critical points to cover and how you will counter any objections.

Are there specific goals you hope the conversation will accomplish? This, of course, depends on the reason for the conversation.

Here's what to keep in mind:

- What is the Number One thing I want to get from this conversation?

- What is the Number One thing he wants to get from this conversation?

- What can we Both get from this conversation? Where is the common ground?

- What else do you want to get from this conversation? It should be a short list.

- If it is about a project or task, how do you want to define the project? What is the deadline you are happy with?

- How will this conversation further or move forward with the relationship you have with this man? What problem(s) will it solve for him, for me, for us as a couple?

Difficult Conversations

Don't go into a difficult conversation without thinking it through.

You need a plan. Be very clear, to yourself, what the problem is, how you will describe the problem, how you will learn how he describes the problem (if he is aware of it yet) and what you hope to accomplish.

Set concrete, measurable goals for yourself and strategies for obtaining these specific goals.

Staging the Conversation -- where and when?

Where you are, as far as environment and locale, can really make the difference.

As women, we may consider what locations are, or could be, romantic.

Otherwise, how much thought do you give to the where and when of conversations?

If not much, could paying attention to this improve your conversation results?

If you want to get to know someone, don't plan on meeting in a loud restaurant, nightclub or at a sporting event unless you are planning minimal conversation.

If you'd like to discuss personal or private subjects, avoid places where you may be easily overheard or interrupted.

If you only plan on topical conversation, a more public area is fine. If you really want to get to know him or talk privately, plan on an appropriate place to do this.

If you're worried that you could run out of things to talk about, get together for a 'doing something' time or date. That could be playing mini-golf or going skating or taking a trial lesson in something together. That way, you have more to talk about.

And Listen So He Will Talk

Chapter Nine

Step 7. You Had Me At "Hello!"

Are you ready to be the first person to say something? Have you always waited for someone else to take control of the situation and lead the direction?

Not anymore!

It is time to jump in and be the first to begin talking and to lead the conversation in the direction you want it to move in.

As a newbie journalist (and a former shy person) I had to learn how to be able to talk to anyone about just about anything. Often, journalists have no choice but to ask difficult questions, in difficult situations.

It wasn't easy, and there are conversations (interviews) that I dreaded, as I know just about every reporter does, when someone is hurt, or someone is in terrible trouble or pain.

It was much more pleasant to do the happy stories about home, families, dogs (loved doing those!) but no reporter ever gets to share only the good news.

And no person only has the easy, happy and warm conversations with people they already know and like.

Start A Conversation With A Man You Haven't Met

First Impressions and the Introduction

First impressions set the tone for the whole relationship forever after.

Allow me to tell you about someone I was absolutely dreading meeting. I was going back to university to get an advanced degree in communications. I had heard that the 'senior prof' I'd be working with (this means helping him in his research; he would also be my thesis advisor and critical to my success) was a cranky old man.

I heard all kinds of stories about him before I met him, because the school I would study at was on the other side of the country from my home.

Oh no, I thought. He's an ogre.

Then, it occurred to me that maybe there was something I could do to change the first impression, and maybe even the whole relationship.

I could change the script.

And to do that, I could start by changing my attitude.

I had a lot of time to think this through during the long drive in a crammed car to the little university town way out West.

The time came to present myself at the office of the friendly Department Head (who had hired me to teach while also earning my degree) who was as wonderful in person as he was on the phone.

He, in turn, would introduce me to Dr. Ogre, my new office-mate.

As we walked there, an older man, perhaps in his 60s, approached. The Department head made the introduction.

I stepped forward, put out my hand to take his in a brief but firm handshake, made eye-contact, and (with a smile in my voice) said, "Dr. Ogre, what a pleasure, I have really been looking forward to meeting you and this opportunity to work with you!" Then, very briefly, I mentioned his work.

Yes, he was surprised. Taken aback, possibly. I did not react to that, because my message was open, honest, ready to work well together. And, critically, ready to form my own opinions about him.

Because a new relationship is always a fresh start.

I'd taken the time to look up his work and know enough about it to be able to talk about it and it did deserve praise.

This professor, on the edge of retirement just as my career was on the edge of launching, would become one of the best and closest friends I have ever had.

What I eventually realized was that he was not "cranky," just frightened and feeling lost after losing his wife (of almost 40 years) and other personal difficulties including ill health that none of his colleagues knew about, because he'd lost the one person he knew how to talk to.

It would be one of most joyful friendships I have ever had, all because we talked. This dear friend is gone now, but rarely does a day go by, decades later, that I don't think about all I learned from him and the many good conversations we shared.

Chapter Ten

Step 8. Keep The Conversation Rolling Right Along

If you're not able to end a conversation, want the conversation to continue or would like to talk about something else, there are several methods or skills that can get you there.

In this chapter, let's look at them:

Staying on Topic

They want to change the topic; you aren't ready to.

You could ask why, or ask when you can talk about that aspect of the topic again, or you could let it go (for now) but get back to it, rephrasing the central idea or theme.

You want to change the topic; they aren't ready to. Just reverse the suggestions in the last paragraph.

Tell them why you want to move on; make a date to get back to that topic.

Conversation rambling – rein that in, as soon as you see his attention wandering or become aware of it as you hear what you're saying.

Re-focus or make a date to continue the conversation; change the topic.

Switching Topics -- If you believe it is time to change the topic of a conversation, ask or tell him you'd like to do that.

You may want to plan on addressing the topic again in the future or you may believe that the topic has been talked to death, but check first. He may feel differently.

The Role of Small Talk

Small talk tends to get a bad rap.

What's small about it is usually the seriousness of the topics – how's your sister doing with her new baby? When is your wife due? Where are you going to school next year? Planning a vacation this summer?

And, of course, how's the weather where you are?

It might seem like fluff (yes, I've heard men call it that) but small talk is conversational lubricant. It fills a very real human need, which is why there isn't a human culture where it does not exist.

As far as we know, humans are the only ones to indulge in small talk.

There are times when we need the relief of lightening the mood, or the moment, with small talk.

Many birds, animals and even plants communicate, but their communication tends to be more immediate and needs-based, as in "Hey, guys, there's food over here!" or "Danger – predator approaching!"

Maybe, in the earliest days of human history, that's about all we had to talk about, too, but somehow I doubt it.

We need serious talk; we also need the relief of lightening it up sometimes with small talk. Just like, sometimes, we need those kittens playing pianos on YouTube to lighten up a dull stretch of working on the computer, or the shop floor.

We need conversation starters that function in the same way that dinner starters do – they whet the appetite (and prepare the brain) for what's to come, the main course conversation.

We need a lighter topic to turn to when the conversation stalls, to recover from embarrassment or difficulty, or, perhaps, to recover our composure and get back on track.

Don't ever underestimate the power of small talk!

The difficulty comes when one person wants to talk small, and the other is ready to talk large.

Non-functional:

    1. Get angry, possibly losing your temper.

2. Roll your eyes, or other signs of impatience (and lack of respect)

3. Insult the other person: "You're such a fool!" "You have no idea what you're talking about!"

4. Always/never statements, such as "You never want to talk anymore" or "All you want to do is tell jokes. Can't you ever be serious?"

5. The "Something's wrong with you message" such as, "Why can't you just lighten up and enjoy the moment?" "Why are you so clumsy/lazy/stupid (etc.)?" Not only is this non-functional, it is abuse, which is the fastest way to destroy trust.

For more insights into small talk, I recommend Shola Kaye's book Big Talk, Small Talk (and Everything In Between).

The Role of Serious Talk

How many people (mostly men or the conversationally-challenged) do you know who leap right into Serious Talk, completely skipping the 'Hi-How are you' warm-up?

It just feels rude, doesn't it?

Yet men aren't the 'only' ones who are prone to leap into serious talk, when small talk first would have been a better choice because it:

1. Helps people relax.

2. Helps make the transition, from work-self to personal life-self or from the way you would talk to a group of people to having a conversation with one specific person.

3. Helps re-connect as two people who are close to each other – or initially send the message (along with appropriate body language) "I'm interested in you."

Forgetting how valuable small talk can be in any relationship can cause arguments and unhappiness that could easily have been avoided with better talk.

Example: Sally's picking her boyfriend at the commuter terminal. He's late. She's been waiting on a hot day, and she's tired after a busy week.

Finally, he arrives, looking just as tired and rumpled as all the other commuters. Sally knows she should use small talk to help them both relax and ease into the beginning of the weekend. But instead, she launches into how she couldn't find a parking space, how long she had to wait for him, why couldn't he have called, work was hell this week…you can see the downward spiral of this conversation. It's going to be difficult to recover from such a bad start to what they both wanted, a great weekend together.

Here's another situation for you to consider: the person who does the opposite. He – or sometimes this is she – never wants to move from small talk to serious talk. They make light of everything. It could be that's how they cope with life, protecting themselves from ever "getting too serious" about anything or anyone. If you are with a person like this who also treats you this way you have to ask yourself, why aren't you 'just friends' because this could be all that this person can ever really be in your life.

Be Specific

Be honest and direct. Don't hint around.

Here's an example: you and your man are walking through a department store. Significant Day (birthday, Christmas, Valentine's Day) is coming up.

You spot a gorgeous sweater on a mannequin.

"Oh, I love this," you say.

As in, hint hint.

Right, he thinks. She likes the sweater.

And then, Significant Day rolls around. He hands you the gift, not shaped at all like it's the sweater.

Nope, it's a certificate for something at a store you don't like.

"I couldn't figure out what to get you," he says. "The guys said their girlfriends all liked getting this."

Disappointment.

It's all downhill from there.

OK, let's hit replay

Store. With man. Spot sweater.

"Love it," you say, but then you add that critical bit of information your man didn't get last time: "If you were thinking about what I'd like as a gift from you for insert-special-day-here, this sweater would be perfect. Size 12 or Medium. The yellow one is my favorite, but I also like the green or the burgundy."

There. You've done it. You didn't hint around (men don't usually get hints), you just plain asked for it and provided all the critical information about size and color options.

From his point of view, there will be no trick questions during the shopping experience.

He can get the sweater.

Or not.

From his point-of-view, he's got the information he needs to solve the problem (gifting opportunity) and reach the big goal (make you happy) so he's a STAR!

Not only is that going to make you happy, you get to enjoy wearing that gorgeous sweater!

Happy Wife, Happy Life – I've heard men say this and then laugh, but there's more than a hint of nervousness about that laugh. They're revealing a deep truth about who they are as well as what they want, which is to accomplish the manly mission of solving problems efficiently and 'making' the most important person in their life happy as a result.

The Magic of an I Message

Do you have something that you believe needs to be said?

State your truth -- facts as well as feelings

Say it clearly and take full responsibility for it.

It's helpful to use the "I message" technique to do this.

Here's how to deliver an I message:

I feel _____, when you_____ because _____. Could you do X instead?

Discussion follows. End it with thanking him for being willing to see your side, acknowledge your feelings and needs, and make a compromise or come to a new understanding.

When the Conversation Lags or Hits a Brick Wall

If you reach an impasse, you need to stop, regroup and look at things from a different perspective.

If emotions are escalating or voices are raised, take the time to regain control of your emotions.

This could also a good time to tell him that you believe there are problems that need a fresh viewpoint and ask for his input.

Handling Awkward Moments

Have you said something that you wish hadn't been said?

Has he?

Be honest and admit it.

It is also possible that a few moments of time-out are called for at this point. A smile, a laugh or even just acknowledging that this isn't easy, can make all the difference in how things progress from here.

Getting to the Conversation Goals and Completing Them

Did you have a list or idea of the goals you wished to accomplish?

Were those goals met?

Sometimes we think we can accomplish much more than is possible in a single conversation.

Remember, you always want to leave them wanting more.

Chapter Eleven

Step 9. Happy Endings

Ok, ask yourself: What is the best possible way this conversation could end?

By now, I think you know the answer. End conversations on a positive note. That creates a desire to get together again.

Some men seem to see conversations as a contest, like a wrestling match, with a "loser" and a "winner." Or they view conversation as getting to the finish line as quickly as possible, like a race.

That can be difficult. It isn't your responsibility to try to change them, but it is your responsibility to get what you need from the conversation and exit pleasantly (or as positively as is possible), dignity intact.

Validating -- what was decided or resolved?

Before you end a conversation that has specific goals, recap what you've discussed and what the conclusions are.

- Do you both believe that the major items are resolved?

- Do you both understand what the other believes and feels?

- Even if you cannot agree, often just letting him know that you understand what he feels and believes can make a difference in how you each perceive the problem or situation or opportunity.

What's Next?

Try to clearly communicate what you would like the next step to be and ask if he agrees.

Don't let it drift away. Set a time to talk again, or accomplish step one and who will do this.

Chapter Twelve

Step 10. Always Exit Smiling

Being able to end a difficult conversation and walk away calmly and with dignity is a skill. It's also a gift you can give yourself.

Ending a conversation that has gone well is much easier than ending a conversation that was a complete disaster. A smile and maybe a hug is much easier than leaving with a bruised ego and an emotional outburst.

Even in the most serious conversation, end with something you agree on, or some up-note of positivity.

Sometimes, we can't help but be angry or upset, but storming away or ending a conversation with an emotional outburst, and especially stomping off, is unproductive.

The rule here: Exit Smiling.

The Power of Positivity

We are surrounded by negative messages in the news, on the Internet, maybe in messages from friends or co-workers or bosses.

And we live in challenging times. No one disputes this.

Straying into negativity is too easy to do. When you focus on the negative, in your job as well as in your personal life and, especially, in your love life, what happens is you begin to miss out on what is good. It's like seeing the world through mud-colored glasses.

And you may fall into some negative ways of thinking, such as thinking in absolutes: You always...you never...

But is this true?

And are things really that bad? What are the facts?

What if you focused on the positives, while trying to do what you can to improve (when you can't eliminate) the negatives?

What if in your conversations and your thinking you could come at issues with a mindset of gratitude for all you have, all that is good, all that is working in your life?

Just changing your attitude to one of positivity gives you more power and more control.

The truth is, there is so much in life we can't control. Our own thoughts, our own reactions, our conversations are all things we CAN control.

Knowing this and choosing to be positive and grateful boosts your confidence, a powerful force in attracting more good relationships and experiences into your life.

Chapter Thirteen

Step 11. Advanced Skillset 1 – Dealing With Difficult Topics

Whether you're talking about vacation plans, money, the kids, family issues, problems at work or at home or what the future holds; using clear, non-accusing, honest facts and openly expressing your thoughts and feelings can make the toughest conversations easier and successful.

When you have to talk about unpleasant subjects, it's important to look at and acknowledge the things that can happen to block communication.

Here are bad habits that can de-rail a challenging conversation:

- Finger-pointing. Don't get sidetracked with whose fault it is

- Anger. This has to do with time and place. Talk when you're both ready to confront the issue, relaxed and in control.

- Denial. One of you just doesn't want to face up to the problem. As a couple, you need to agree that if one person sees a given issue as serious, it IS serious.

And here's what can help:

- Can you state what the problem is clearly? Can you boil it down to one sentence? Can you state the problem in a way that is blame-neutral?

- Can you keep the problem in the NOW?

- Can you speak without placing blame?

- Can you state how you are feeling or the impact this problem is having on you (and anyone else directly involved) without being aggressive?

- Can you listen to what he has to say and ask for suggestions or ideas without being overly emotional?

- Are you prepared to react calmly if he becomes emotional?

- Brainstorming is a good way to begin resolving the problem. You both list all ideas that could solve the problem, no matter how far-fetched, and write them all down without making any judgements yet. Then you use those ideas to act as a foundation for searching for the best solution out of all your possible options.

- Asking others for assistance, input or ideas can also be helpful, but should only be done if both of you agree.

How to Talk About Bad News

It's no one's favorite task to have to have to deliver bad news. Do it in the most compassionate way possible.

This should be in private and in person.

Don't start with a build-up, don't dramatize, don't use emotional language, don't emphasize the negative.

Be short and concise. Just state what has happened, what happens now and, if appropriate, what happens next.

Offer your care and kindness. Don't downplay the importance of the news or situation, don't suggest that you "know exactly" how they feel, because you probably can't and don't.

Don't tell him it could be worse or that you have experienced things that were worse and then start to talk about those bad things that happened to you.

Being there for someone, offering your kindness, being willing to listen if they want to talk, or to allow that person to have space and silence are the best things you can give to help the grieving, which is the first step in healing, begin.

Chapter Fourteen

Step 12. Advanced Skillset 2 – Dealing With Difficult Men

He's dashing, he's handsome, he's exciting to be with and, sometimes or maybe a lot of the time, he's difficult, but you love him.

And you need to talk to him.

All of the tips and techniques we've already talked about are your tools for any conversation with anyone, including people who are difficult.

One or both of you is unloving as well as failing to communicate effectively in these ways:

- Shouting rather than talking

- Abusive, swearing
- Dishonest, deceitful
- Manipulative, controlling or threatening
- Bullying
- Violent
- Using put-downs
- Showing contempt
- Constantly critical, never pleased.
- Negative
- Totally self-involved, ignoring the needs or feelings of others.

If this is happening, you have more than a communication problem. I urge you to get qualified help from a certified therapist or counsellor. Do NOT put this off, because you are living in a dangerous situation.

Your doctor, spiritual advisor or a trusted friend will be able to recommend someone with the skills and experience to help you get to a better place in your life.

If how to pay for help is a concern, your health insurance may cover counselling. Some workplaces also offer counselling or therapy when needed in their compensation package. Look into what resources are available, make the call and get the help and support you need.

If He's Your Ex

My sister's ex is a good person. I'm happy that he's still in our lives, because before they married, he was a good friend of my husband's and that's still true.

Fortunately, my sister understands that we wouldn't take sides when they split up.

They had the intelligence and the basic caring for each other that their divorce was one of the most civilized I know of personally. That was good for them and especially good for the child (and now, grandchildren) they share, as well as a relief to all the family members and friends who care about both of them.

But it doesn't always turn out this way. Breaking up well takes skill, compassion, tolerance and patience. At an emotional time it calls on us to be rational.

Dealing with exes, especially when you parted in anger as well as disappointment, can be very painful and make for some awful conversations after that.

So, if you need to talk to an ex and you know you are still very emotional about the break-up but the conversation is unavoidable (if you share parenting responsibilities, for example), my advice is to keep every conversation short, focused and problem-solving.

Take the emotionality out of it.

Make it fact-based and emotions-neutral, as much as possible. And keep it in the present.

Chapter Fifteen

Wishing You Many Happy Conversations…

Ok, let's take just a few minutes to review.

Poor communication techniques are learned behaviours and habits, usually formed in childhood and possibly reinforced by our culture. This is good news, because you can recognize behaviours that don't work and replace them with better techniques and habits that work much better.

You don't have to dwell on what happened in the past. The past doesn't dictate what will happen now or in the future.

Generally speaking, men and women communicate differently.

Women seem to be able to talk about casual subjects and more profound subjects with relative ease just about anywhere to just about any other woman.

Men, on the other hand, will communicate differently when in a group of men, when women are present and when alone with a trusted friend.

This means that women need to learn what subjects are interesting to men and to the specific man, depending on the environment.

Women are also more prone to express their emotions than men. Many men find this mystifying, or it makes them upset and angry because they see this as irrational behaviour. They can't process it; therefore, it's threatening. They need help understanding, but you also need to understand their preferred ways of talking and listening.

In this book, I provided many tools for better communication, and I will list them here:

1. The Rule of Three – tell what you're going to tell them. Tell them. Tell them what you just told them. Don't repeat.

2. The "I message" - I feel _____, when you_____ because _____. Could you do X instead ….thank you.

3. Giving feedback – "So, what I heard you say is ___, is that correct?"

4. Don't order - Ask

5. Wait to respond (the pause that refreshes!)

6. Understand the difference between feelings and thoughts

7. Thoughts are beliefs - Does he share them, or disagree?

8. Make eye contact (unless you're in Asia!)

9. Time and place matter

10. Have a ready smile and a positive attitude

11. As much as possible, say it in a positive way, rather than a negative (defeated) way

12. Ask for what you want and need. Ask him what he wants and needs. Lovers aren't mind-readers.

Remember this about men

- They want to protect the women they care about.

- They need to solve problems.

- Facts and logic are their comfort zone.

- Lacking a rich emotional language, they tend to distrust emotion-talk and body language. Some men are threatened by emotion-talk or behaviour.

- Most men tend towards a literal translation of any message.

- They want and need to be seen as your hero, truly your Knight in Shining Armour.

- They believe they have an Important Life Mission, and need to find it and excel at it (almost always this is career or a very strong avocation that, perhaps, should have been their career).

- They want to make you happy, so they can be happy.

- Woman they are close to are their conduit – sometimes their only conduit – to their deepest emotions, their essential being.

- They see the world as practical, a list of facts, problems to be solved through ingenuity and intelligence as well as creativity and that is how they think and how they talk.

- Yes, they are entirely capable of subtleties of meaning, of inference and even of interpreting gestures and body language – they just don't often do these things because they don't *believe* in them. They don't put much credence or value on body language, therefore missing its messages.

- They don't send 'signals,' they talk. To them, what they say is what they mean. There is no hidden subtext, no secret language of guys, no guy-conspiracy.

- When they seem tentative, they are out of this male comfort zone (facts, problems) and may appear to be cold (to women) when the truth is they are just on (what is to them) shaky ground or that scary planet called Feelings.

- If you just want to explore possibilities or vent or cry on his shoulder or get his support, tell him. Be very clear about what you want and need.

- Listening isn't agreeing. You don't have to always agree with someone in order to love them or like them, but you do have to listen with respect for their outlook and opinions, without interrupting.

If you come away from our time together as you read this book with only three thoughts, let them be these:

1. Men fix problems to make their world make sense

2. Women nurture relationships to make their world make sense

3. Men and women have more in common than differences. Both want to be needed, listened to, understood and cherished.

Wishing you many warm and satisfying conversations... no matter where life love and your relationships take you...

Before You Go...

Just one Last Thing...

If you believe it's well worth sharing, could you take a moment or two to leave a review where you bought this book (if you bought it online) and let your friends on social know about it?

If it helps your friends and others communicate better with the man (and the men) in their lives, and especially with the man they long to get closer to, they'll be grateful to you.

And so will I.

Wishing you MANY satisfying conversations!

-Jacquelyn

About Jacquelyn

Jacquelyn Elnor Johnson has written more than 20 non-fiction books, both under her own name and as the ghostwriter. During her three decades as a journalist, she was a reporter, photographer, newspaper and magazine editor and publisher.

She has also taught journalism and marketing to college and university students and ESL to children ages 8 to 17.

Her hundreds of articles have appeared in Los Angeles Times, Toronto Star, Hamilton Spectator and Canadian Business, among dozens of newspapers and magazines.

She holds a B.A. in English from Millersville University in Pennsylvania, a M.S. in Journalism and Communications from South Dakota State University and a MBA from Wilfrid Laurier University in Ontario, Canada.

www.ingramcontent.com/pod-product-compliance
Lightning Source LLC
Chambersburg PA
CBHW071450070526
44578CB00001B/294